THIS BOOK BELONGS TO

101 Beautiful Patterns Coloring Book

Thank you for purchasing this quality adult coloring book from Cottage Path Press!

Inside this volume are 101 beautiful coloring page designs with varying levels of intricacy. You'll find everything from florals and mandalas, to animals and sea life, and various images of beauty and whimsy—all awaiting your creativity and artistic flair.

Each image is on its own page with a blank back side to help avoid color bleed-through. If you use something other than colored pencils or crayons, we also recommend placing a sheet of paper or some other blotter between your coloring page and the one beneath it while you work. To test your colors, use the testing page provided at the back of this book.

We hope you enjoy your Cottage Path Press Coloring Book!

MORE COLORING BOOKS FOR ADULTS
101 Beautiful Patterns Vol. 2
101 Amazing Mandalas
Pretty Easy Mandalas
Favorite Bible Verses
50 Fabulous Mandalas
Simply Soothing Mandalas
Beautiful Flowers

BONUS! Look for a FREE printables offer at the end of this book!

PAGE 1

PAGE 2

PAGE 3

PAGE 4

PAGE 5

PAGE 7

PAGE 8

PAGE 9

PAGE 10

PAGE 11

PAGE 12

PAGE 13

PAGE 15

PAGE 19

PAGE 20

PAGE 21

PAGE 22

PAGE 23

PAGE 25

PAGE 26

PAGE 28

PAGE 29

PAGE 30

PAGE 31

PAGE 32

PAGE 33

PAGE 35

PAGE 36

PAGE 37

PAGE 38

PAGE 39

PAGE 40

PAGE 41

PAGE 42

PAGE 43

PAGE 44

PAGE 45

PAGE 48

PAGE 49

PAGE 51

PAGE 52

PAGE 53

PAGE 54

PAGE 55

PAGE 56

PAGE 57

PAGE 58

PAGE 59

PAGE 60

PAGE 61

PAGE 62

PAGE 63

PAGE 64

PAGE 65

PAGE 66

PAGE 67

PAGE 68

PAGE 69

PAGE 70

PAGE 71

PAGE 72

PAGE 73

PAGE 74

PAGE 75

PAGE 76

PAGE 77

PAGE 78

PAGE 80

PAGE 81

PAGE 82

PAGE 83

PAGE 84

PAGE 85

PAGE 86

PAGE 87

PAGE 88

PAGE 89

PAGE 90

PAGE 91

PAGE 92

PAGE 93

PAGE 94

PAGE 95

PAGE 96

PAGE 97

PAGE 99

PAGE 100

PAGE 101

We'd love to hear how you liked this book!

Please show your support for our small family business and help other colorists discover our books by leaving a review for this title on Amazon.

   **THANK YOU!**

GET FREE COLORING PAGE PRINTABLES FROM COTTAGE PATH PRESS!

To sign up for bonus coloring pages, type the URL below into your browser, then follow the instructions.

http://bit.ly/101BCP

Don't miss these other books available from Cottage Path Press

Books for Kids

Color Testing Page

Made in the USA
Las Vegas, NV
30 October 2022